Easter Sunday

WEEK ONE

FOR LEADERS

Easter Sunday isn't simply a happy ending to the story of Jesus life - it is a new, joyful beginning!

This week introduces the series and why we'll be reflecting on the resurrection for seven weeks. It makes the point that Jesus' rising from the dead changed everything: for the two Marys, the disciples, and the whole world.

We've intentionally given you lots of songs for this week, to emphasise celebration and introduce material you can re-use as the weeks progress.

GATHERING

Gathering Prayer

LEADER: Christ is risen!
ALL: He is risen indeed, hallelujah!

Into our darkness dawns your light.
Out of the grave your glory shines.
Jesus, you meet us, risen saviour,
and we respond in delighted worship.

Christ is risen!
He is risen indeed, hallelujah!

Intro Poem Video

This sets the scene for both Easter Morning and the whole Resurrection People series.

ALL AGE IDEAS

Game: Egg Surprise

Tell the children that there are small chocolate Easter Eggs hidden around the room (show one as an example), and that they need to go and find them.

After a minute or so of people fruitlessly searching, admit that actually there are no eggs hidden. Ask people how they feel at this news. Sad? Disappointed? Frustrated? Confused? Explain that this is what Jesus' friends felt when they went to the tomb, but his body wasn't there.

Then say that, rather than the small eggs, you actually have bigger, better chocolate eggs for all the children. Ask them how they feel now. Excited? Surprised? Happy? Get them to think about what Jesus' friends felt when they realised that his body was not in the tomb because he had risen from the dead. Then give out the eggs!

Song: Easter Doesn't Stop

The video of this fun song is a great way to help all ages catch the idea that Easter isn't just a day. Lead sheet printed on page 39. Engage everyone in the actions as demonstrated by Gemma in the video.

but Easter doesn't stop there.

Scribble Sheets

For each week you can download scribble sheets designed for children. You could use these in Children's Church, or give them out after an All Age service, or any other way that works in your setting.

MUSIC IDEAS

Song: He's Not Here

This performance song helps you remember that alongside joy and celebration there is also a note of sadness and "blues" on Easter Day. You could reflect around the idea that we all wrestle with the two truths - "he's not here" and yet "he is here".

Song: Draw Near The Tomb (Resurrection Day)

This worship song journeys through the resurrection story from Matthew 28. It touches on lots of the themes of this series, so is worth learning and using as a theme song. Sheet music is printed on page 38, or make use of the video pictured below.

"He is not here. He is risen from the dead. Come see the stone is rolled away."

Songs

- *Draw Near The Tomb (Resurrection Day)* - Sam Hargreaves (page 38)
- *Easter Doesn't Stop* - Timo Scharnowski (page 39)
- *In Christ, New Creation* - Sam Hargreaves (page 40)
- *Christ Was Raised* - Sam Hargreaves (page 43)
- *Forever* - Kari Jobe
- *Christ is Risen, Indeed* - Matt Boswell

Hymns:

- *Thine Be The Glory* - Edmond Budry, Richard Hoyle
- *Christ The Lord Is Risen Today* - Charles Wesley
- *I Know That My Redeemer Lives* - Samuel Medley, John Hatton
- *Crown Him With Many Crowns* - Matthew Bridges, Godfrey Thring

 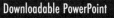

HEARING GOD'S WORD

Bible Readings

Matthew 28:1-10
2 Corinthians 5:16-21

Matthew 28:1-10 Interactive

Read the passage, and get the congregation to repeat the actions/phrases. You could have two people lead this, one as the reader and one leading the actions.

It was dawn on Sunday morning [*stretch and yawn*].

The day after Saturday, which itself was the day after Good Friday [*put out your arms like Jesus on the cross*].

Mary One [*put up one finger*] and Mary Two [*put up a finger on the other hand*] went to the tomb [*make your two fingers walk along*].

Suddenly [*say "gasp"*] there was a violent earthquake [*shake your whole body*].

An angel came from heaven and rolled the stone away from the tomb [*mime pushing away a big stone*].

He looked like lightning [*say "kapow"*] and his outfit was as white as snow [*say "how does he keep it clean?"*].

The guards were so afraid they shook [*shake your whole body*].

The angel said to the women "Do not be afraid" [*say "do not be afraid"*].

"You're looking for Jesus, who was crucified" [*put out your arms like Jesus on the cross*].

"He is not here, he has risen" [*Say, "he's risen indeed, hallelujah!"*].

"Come and see, the place he was laying is empty" [*make spectacles with your fingers and look*].

"Then go quickly and tell his disciples - he has risen" [*say, "he's risen indeed, hallelujah!"*].

So the women ran to the disciples [*mime running*], afraid [*mime biting nails*] yet filled with joy [*shout "yippee!"*].

Suddenly [*say "gasp"*] Jesus met them [*put out your arms like Jesus on the cross*].

Mary One [*put up one finger*] and Mary Two [*put up a finger on the other hand*] bent over, grasping his feet and worshipping him [*make your two fingers bend over and say "he's risen indeed, hallelujah!"*].

Jesus said "Do not be afraid" [*say "do not be afraid"*].

"Go and tell my brothers to go to Galilee, there they will see me" [*one more time, say "he's risen indeed, hallelujah!"*]

Sermon Outline

Expand upon the following, exploring the passages. For further input read this week's Personal Devotions, and we also recommend "This Risen Existence" by Paula Gooder.

A spectator or a participant?
[*This illustration can be adapted to reflect a recent sports event.*] You can watch a sports event like the Olympics or the World Cup, and be happy when your team win or sad when they lose. Ultimately, as a spectator, your life will go on relatively unchanged. But if you are a participant, if you yourself compete in that event and you win, it changes you. You have a new outlook on the world, a new title - World Champion, Gold Medallist, Fastest in the World... and your life will never be the same.

The Marys were transformed (Matt 28:1-10)
The two Marys were not mere spectators on that first Easter Day. Jesus was their close friend, their teacher, their Lord. They thought he was dead, they thought all their hopes and dreams had been shattered. Then the earth shook, the stone was rolled away, and the angel showed them the world-changing truth: "He is not here; he has risen." This transforms them. They go from mourners to worshippers. They respond to Jesus by getting on their knees in love and devotion. And then he sends

For all free downloads plus song and hymn links, visit www.engageworship.org/resurrection using password on page 2.

5

them as the first witnesses to his risen life. They go as missionaries, as witnesses of all they have seen and heard, heralds of Jesus who was dead and is now gloriously alive.

Will we be spectators, or Resurrection People?
Paul writes:

> "just as Christ was raised from the dead through the glory of the Father, we too may live a new life. For if we have been united with him in a death like his, we will certainly also be united with him in a resurrection like his." (Rom 6:4-5)

It is possible to be a spectator to Easter. To enjoy the eggs and the flowers, the songs and the celebration, and then go away unchanged. Or we can be participants, with skin in the game. Like the two Marys, we can be transformed by meeting the risen Jesus.

New Creation is here
Jesus' resurrection is the beginning of God's restoration plan for everything he made - the making new of all creation. In another place, Paul writes: "Therefore, if anyone is in Christ, the new creation has come: The old has gone, the new is here!" (2 Cor 5:17). We have been raised with Jesus as part of that new creation. We can be Resurrection People, who see the whole world differently, and live to bring God's reconciliation and restoration to the situations around us. Easter is more than a day. Today we're kicking off the seven week celebration of Eastertide where we'll be exploring this in more depth. But more importantly, if we allow it to be, Easter is the beginning of a whole new life with the risen Jesus.

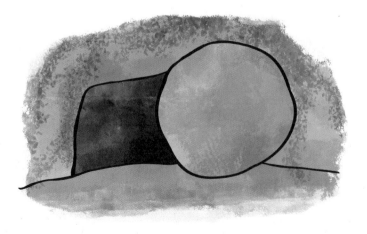

RESPONSE
Coming To Faith

It may well feel right to offer people the chance to become Christians at this service, and also for people to make re-commitments. Below is a prayer you could use. Remember to invite people to follow-up conversations or courses.

God, I believe that you made me and you love me. I want to trust my life into your hands.

Jesus, I believe you died for me on that first Good Friday. I trust that my old life of selfishness and sin died on the cross with you. The old has gone, the new has come.

I believe that you rose to new life on Easter Sunday. You say that I am raised with you, a new creation, and that my life and my eternity is in your hands.

Holy Spirit, as you raised Jesus from the dead, fill me now with that resurrection power. May I live for you in all I do, sharing your love with others, bringing your kingdom in this world, until you come again.

Amen.

Contemplative Response: Agents of Reconciliation

This is an imaginative reflection, helping us to think through what the world would look like if we took seriously our calling to be God's Agents of Reconciliation (2 Cor 5). It ends with space for people to listen to God and apply this to their own circumstances.

I want to invite you for a moment to close your eyes and imagine an alternative reality.

In our reality, in our society, the stories that surround us are about division and wars:

The rebels in one country violently oppose the legally elected government, leading to bloodshed and another refugee crisis.

The Left side and the Right side of our own parliaments are at constant loggerheads, voting down each others' plans.

Church denominations split in two, or maybe more, over one or two lines in their creeds.

The board of directors at your company votes to sack the CEO, because he said something they disagreed with.

The tabloids report on the ongoing feuds between celebrities, major and minor... [*Download full text via engageworship.org/resurrection*]

Active Response: Throw Out The Old

You will need: Pile of rubbish (clean to touch but clearly trash - crisp packets, empty drinks bottles etc would be good). Rubbish bin(s). Download and printout cards with the verse on.

Explain: Paul writes this to the Corinthians:

> "Therefore, if anyone is in Christ, the new creation has come: The old has gone, the new is here!"

Do you ever leave things that you know you really should throw out? Rubbish that really needs to go in the bin? Junk that piles up waiting to go to the dump? Old food that lingers at the back of the fridge, growing mouldy?

This happens in our hearts as well as our homes. We can let old, out-of-date thoughts, attitudes and feelings hang around, because we're too busy or lazy or scared to deal with them. But after a while, they start taking up room and maybe even begin to smell.

Maybe it is a way of behaving which you know is not right, but you can't seem to kick the habit. Or a way of thinking about yourself that you know isn't true, but you haven't fully left it behind. It could be an unforgiven resentment towards someone else, or a disappointment that you know you need to move on from.

Remember: if you're in Christ, the new creation has come in your life. The old is gone. So it's time to let go of those old, stinky things.

We've got a pile of rubbish here. In the next few moments, we'd love to invite you to come and pick up a piece of rubbish (don't worry, it's clean), and hold it in your hand, thinking about what it represents for you. Then give that thing over to God, and symbolically put that in the rubbish bin.

Then you can take one of these cards and put it somewhere you will notice it, to remind you that you're a new creation.

Song: In Christ, New Creation

This is based on the 2 Corinthians 5 passage about our calling as agents of reconciliation. Lead sheet printed on page 40, actions and lyric videos downloadable.

We're rising to his call.

SENDING

Sending Prayer

LEADER: God sends you out
to be his resurrection people!

Jesus who was dead, is now alive.
ALL: And we are his witnesses.

The old is gone, the new is here.
And we are a new creation.

God reconciles the world to himself in Christ.
And we are his ambassadors.

**God, send us out
to be your resurrection people!**

Renewing Joy

WEEK TWO

FOR LEADERS

There is a tradition going back hundreds of years, and observed across the world, celebrating the second Sunday of Easter as "Bright Sunday" or "Holy Humour" Sunday. This can involve parties, picnics, jokes, and other fun ways to celebrate the resurrection with joy.

This week, encourage laughter and fun in your service, in whatever way that is appropriate for your congregation. Don't buy into the idea that church should be dour and that our joy should be so deep it never reaches our faces. Don't perpetuate the myth that happiness and joy are different - the Bible never makes this distinction. The root of true happiness is in God's love for us, and joy and laughter can be triggered by recognising all kinds of good gifts around us - colours, jokes, food, silly things and serious things. Give people permission to enjoy themselves this Sunday.

"Laughter is carbonated holiness."

Anne Lamott, Plan B, page 66.

GATHERING

Gathering Prayer

LEADER: Christ is risen!
ALL: He is risen indeed, hallelujah!

However we come, in excitement or tears,
you meet us all and bring us joy.
Lift our spirits, risen saviour,
help us hear you speak our name.

Christ is risen!
He is risen indeed, hallelujah!

Confession Prayer

Jesus, you were filled with joy in the Holy Spirit,
you delighted in the company of laughing children,
you told funny stories and enjoyed a good party.

Forgive us when we confuse holiness with being humourless.
Sometimes we take ourselves too seriously, and fail to see the funny side.
We can miss out on childlike joy and wide-eyed wonder in this world you've made.

Help us to live lightly in your resurrection power,

filled with the joy of our salvation,
grateful for what we have and content whatever our circumstances.

Help us to rejoice with those who rejoice,
mourn with those who mourn,
giggle uncontrollably with those who giggle uncontrollably,
and be bringers of your good, happy news to the world.

Amen.

ALL AGE IDEAS

Dance Party

Decorate your worship space for a fun and colourful party - balloons, streamers, banners and so on. Encourage your musicians to play joyful music, and invite people to dance.

If your congregation is really relaxed, you could have a "dance off" where volunteers dance for 30 seconds and the person who gets the biggest cheer wins a prize. (Remember, none of this has to be serious or make a "point", other than that it is a good thing to celebrate and have fun in God's presence together.)

Joke Share

Ask people to come ready to share a favourite joke (you might want them to tell the joke to a leader first just to check for appropriateness!) Encourage children to tell their jokes, but also open it up to all ages.

Bubble Prayers

You will need: Soap bubble kits of liquid and wands, enough for the size of the congregation.

Ask people to think of one person or situation they want to pray for, that God would bring them joy. Get people to say aloud the name of that person or situation, and then to blow into a bubble wand and make soap bubbles. These symbolise our prayers rising up to God. In a larger gathering, you can get people into groups and give each group a bubble kit.

Emoji Responses

To highlight that it's OK to feel a range of emotions, have a moment in the beginning of the service where you ask the congregation to express how they've felt in their week, using emojis only. You could make it simple, by putting the service leader's phone number on the screen or service sheet, and then simply reading the responses out "Someone here has been very happy; Jean has sent a cold emoji; Kevin has been sad..." etc.

Or if you have the technical ability and good internet connection in the church, you could use an online, interactive tool like Mentimeter, Swipe or Participoll. Why not get some teenagers to help you set it up?

Peter's Slowcoach Blues

A bluesy rendition of John and Peter running to the tomb, imagining Peter's indignation at how John tells the tale!

MUSIC IDEAS

Songs

- *Happy Day* - Tim Hughes, Ben Cantelon
- *Joy* - Rend Collective
- *Joy* - For King & Country
- *Joyful (The One Who Saves)* - Brenton Brown
- *Lord It's Hard To Recognise You* - Sam Hargreaves (page 41)
- *Go Tell The World (Mary Magdalene's Song)* - Philippa Hanna, Chris Eaton, Kyle Lee
- *See What A Morning* - Stuart Townend

Hymns:

- *That Easter Day With Joy Was Bright -* trans. JM Neale
- *Joy Dawned Again On Easter Day -* trans. JM Neale
- *Comes Mary To The Grave -* Michael Perry
- *See Your Hands Overflowing With Flowers -* trans. Christopher Idle
- *The Lord Is Here, The Darkness Gone -* Christopher Idle

HEARING GOD'S WORD

Bible Readings

John 20:1-18
John 16:20-24
Psalm 126

Easter Drama

By Dave Hopwood

This draws on Matt 27:51-53, 28:1-10 and John 20:1-18. It is a funny but still impactful way of conveying the resurrection. Below we have printed the opening scene, download the full script online.

Cast: Narrator, Pilate, Sleeping soldier/s, 2 Angels, Mary, a group of 3 or 4 women, 3 "Dead" People, Peter and John. It is vital that the audience have no idea who is playing Jesus until the very end of this piece. If possible, have two angels hidden somewhere on or near the stage area before beginning.

[Enter Pilate, he takes a moment to walk up and down, eyeing the audience before speaking.]

Pilate: All right you lot! Pilate here. I'm in charge, now listen up. So, you want to go and see the body? What good will that do? It's over. Why are you just prolonging the agony. Accept the truth — your leader's dead. I saw him with my own eyes. It's no good pretending. Whatever he might have told you before, he's gone now. Move on. There's nothing to see.

I've appointed soldiers at the tomb, so it's dangerous, I don't want strangers tramping all over the place. There'll be trouble. There'll be a riot. You should just go back to bed. Go on... *[Download full text via engageworship.org/resurrection]*

Pass the Parcel

If children are staying in for the reading, you could play the British party game "pass the parcel". Print out John 20:1-18 two verses at a time (so they are on 9 slips of paper). Gift wrap verses 17-18 along with a sweet or other small prize. Continue to wrap the verses and prizes in further layers around the first one, until verses 1-2 are in the final layer.

Play music, and have the congregation pass the parcel from person to person. When it stops, the person holding the parcel opens a layer of wrapping paper and reads the verses aloud (if they're very shy they could get someone near them to read).

Psalm 126: Active Version

You can teach the singing part - the line from the Pharrell Williams song "Happy" - beforehand. For the rest, just get people to repeat after you.

When the Lord brought us back from exile [*make beckoning, "come here" hand motion*],

it felt like we were dreaming [*stretch and yawn, then look amazed*].

Our mouths were filled with laughter [*laugh*],

our tongues with songs of joy [*sing: "because I'm Happy"*].

Then it was said among the nations [*cup hands around mouth*],

"The Lord has done great things for them" [*say "the Lord has done great things for them", pointing away at "them"*].

The Lord has done great things for us [*say "the Lord has done great things for us", pointing towards yourself at "us"*]

and we are filled with joy [*sing: "because I'm Happy"*].

Restore our fortunes, Lord, [*put arms out to receive*]

like streams in the desert [*say "ahh, that's refreshing!"*].

Those who sow with tears [*mime crying*]

will reap with songs of joy [*sing: "because I'm Happy"*],

those who go out weeping [*mime crying*]

carrying seed to sow [*mime throwing seed around*]

will return with songs of joy [*sing: "because I'm Happy"*],

carrying sheaves with them [*mime carrying bundle*].

Sermon Outline

Expand upon the following, exploring the passages. For further input read this week's Personal Devotions, and we also recommend "Emotionally Healthy Spirituality" by Pete Scazzero.

How happy and sad can we be?

How do you feel about joy, laughter and happiness? For some Christians these things feel irreverent, silly, childish or pointless. We seem to forget that Jesus himself was filled with joy (Luke 10:21), and that God's people laugh and sing happy songs (Ps 126:2). Equally, other people will feel that expressing pain, sadness or grief is somehow inappropriate for a believer, forgetting that Jesus wept (John 11:35) and that Christians continue to experience struggle in this life (2 Cor 1:8). In ignoring the range of our feelings we can end up living in a bland, beige middle ground, never fully allowing the deep mourning or exuberant happiness that are healthy, human and holy emotions.

Jesus promises grief and rejoicing

When he is foretelling his death and resurrection, Jesus tells his disciples that they will experience weeping and mourning, and that their grief will turn to joy (John 16:20-24). This echoes Psalm 126, where it suggests that expressing sorrow is like sowing seed, which leads to a harvest of joy (126:5). We're invited into both the sadness of Good Friday and the wholehearted celebration of Easter. Our lives can echo both the cross and the resurrection, the weeping and the laughing.

Tears and laughter at the resurrection

In John 20:11-17 we see this range of emotions in Mary Magdalene. To begin with she is weeping at having lost her Lord and friend. By the end, she is filled with irrepressible joy. This pattern happens in many of the resurrection encounters - mourning turns to dancing, tears to smiles. Jesus accepts all of these emotions. The resurrection is the truest source of lasting joy. It gives us a foretaste of what eternity with God will be like. However, until Jesus returns, we will live holding the tension of this joy with the realities of sadness, pain and struggle. Easter invites us to embrace and express both.

Owning our emotions in our lives

What would it look like for us to be honest about the full range of our emotions: in our personal lives, our prayer lives, and our church worship? When we are with our friends, families and work colleagues, what would it look like to "Rejoice with those who rejoice; mourn with those who mourn." (Rom 12:15)? To be real about pain, sadness and grief? To celebrate our eternal hope in the resurrected Jesus, and truly enjoy every good gift we are given in the meantime, however big or small, silly or serious?

RESPONSE

Contemplative Response: Open Our Eyes

Lead the following slowly and reflectively.

Mary looked at Jesus, but she didn't recognise him. She mistook him for a stranger, a gardener, someone who had carried Jesus away.

Then he said her name, and suddenly her eyes were opened. Her sorrow turned to joy. A hopeless situation suddenly beamed with hope. The absent Jesus was suddenly present.

Think about your daily life - your home, your job, a situation in your family or community. Is there a place where things feel hopeless? Where it feels like Jesus is absent? Picture that situation in your mind. How does it feel to be there? What are your questions to God in that place?

Now, imagine that as you are in that place, Jesus speaks your name. He makes himself known to you. He shows you that he is in that situation. Where is Jesus in that place? How does he relate to you and the other people around you?

Active: Sowing With Tears, Reaping With Joy

Hand out small seeds. Have some soil in pots accessible around the room. You may also want to point out towards the end of this activity that if people are struggling with big issues they can also access prayer ministry or pastoral care - you don't want people to "bury" their problems without seeking help.

Read: Psalm 126:5-6:

> Those who sow with tears
> will reap with songs of joy.
> Those who go out weeping,
> carrying seed to sow,
> will return with songs of joy,
> carrying sheaves with them.

Explain: Sometimes, expressing our sorrow acts like planting a seed. Until we have expressed our difficult emotions, it can be difficult to reap a harvest of joy. God wants us to be real with him, to come to him with whatever we are thinking or feeling. Bottling up pain, anger, doubts or other struggles can stop us from receiving God's healing and restoration.

Hold this seed in your hand, and think about struggles you are experiencing. Are there painful experiences where you have been hurt by another person, or you feel disappointed with God, or regretful of how you have acted? God is big enough to hear your heart, to receive how you feel. As much as you feel able, speak to God honestly about those things... [*Download full text via engageworship. org/resurrection*]

Song: Lord It's Hard To Recognise You

This song puts us in the position of Mary, the Emmaus pair and Thomas, who all fail to recognise or believe in the risen Jesus at their first opportunity. You can play the video or have musicians lead this live. It may work to encourage people just to listen to the song first, and only join in towards the end.

SENDING

Sending Prayer

LEADER: God sends you out
to be his resurrection people!

Jesus who was dead, is now alive.
ALL: He turned our grief into joy.

Jesus wept, and Jesus laughed.
We weep with him and laugh with him.

God sends us out to weep with those who mourn and rejoice with those who rejoice.
We go out into a needy world.

**God, send us out
to be your resurrection people!**

Restructuring Imagination

FOR LEADERS

The travellers to Emmaus felt like their world had ended. They couldn't picture a crucified Messiah, they didn't believe that someone could rise again. It took an encounter with Jesus to restructure their imaginations. They began to see the whole world through new eyes, through resurrection lenses.

We have included a format for an Emmaus Holy Communion as part of this week.

GATHERING

Gathering Prayer

LEADER: Christ is risen!
ALL: He is risen indeed, hallelujah!

Meet with us and walk with us,
open your word, break the bread.
May we see you, risen saviour,
warm our hearts with your living presence.

Christ is risen!
He is risen indeed, hallelujah!

Resurrection Imagination

This is a fun all-age talk, which invites people to de-code "secret messages" on the screen, and think about the lenses through which we look at the world. You will need to hand out pieces of red cellophane, or if you're feeling really crafty you could make glasses with the cellophane for lenses.

Ask: Look at this. Can you see what it is? How about with the red cellophane?

How about this. Can you read it?

CONFUSING MESSAGES

How about these?

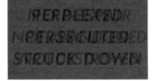

These words were written by Paul in the Bible. What does that last one mean? How do you look at what you can't see? [*Invite answers.*]

We've used these red bits of cellophane to see what we can't normally see. In other circumstances, you could use technology like an X-ray machine to see inside a body, a thermal imager to see heat and cold, or a microscope to see very tiny things. But there is another way, that doesn't involve machinery. We can use our imagination.

Ask: How do you use your imagination? [*Writing stories. Lego or Minecraft. Daydreaming. Creating music...*]... [*Download full text online.*]

MUSIC IDEAS

Songs

- *Lord It's Hard To Recognise You* - Sam Hargreaves (page 41)
- *Open Our Eyes* - Zac Hicks, Bruce Benedict
- *O Hidden One* - Pillar Church
- *Remembrance (The Communion Song)* - Matt Redman, Matt Maher
- *Abide With Me* - David Crowder, Jason Ingram, Matt Maher, Matt Redman

Hymns:

- *Two Companions Journeyed Homeward* - Emma Turl
- *As We Walk Along Beside You* - Michael Perry
- *O Lord Whose Love Designed This Day* - Christopher Idle

HEARING GOD'S WORD

Bible Readings

Luke 24:13-35
2 Corinthians 4:7-18

Emmaus Poem: In Disguise

By Dave Hopwood

While they were walking together he drew near
in disguise, quietly listening, unnoticed for a time.
While they were talking together
he came alongside,
available, interested,
inquiring about their conversation.

"Don't you know?" they said, "are you oblivious?"
He smiled, "Tell me about it," he said.
And so they did, as they walked together,
and he quietly listened, in disguise, taking it all in.

And so they talked and he listened,
nodding at news he already knew,
already understood on a much deeper level,
and when they had finished he spoke, in disguise.

And he took them back in time,
back through history and the prophets,
back through pain and trouble and longing,
back to the dawning of a plan.

And so they stopped for food and he broke bread,
as he had done with them only days before.
He lifted the bread in disguise
and lowered it as Jesus of Nazareth,
resurrected one.

And as their eyes were opened,
he disappeared. No more need for disguise,
no more need to be there in that place.
And so they ran back to their friends.

No more escaping, no more fleeing.
And as they told their story he drew near again.
And so it is today,
Jesus of Nazareth often walks close,
in disguise, resurrected, listening,
understanding, available.

Sermon Outline

Expand upon the following, exploring the passages. For further input read this week's Personal Devotions, and the passage on Emmaus in "Sacred Fire" by Ronald Rolheiser.

Imagination is a precious gift

New, innovative buildings are put up because of the imagination of the architect. Families relocate to other parts of the world because they can dream of a new life there. Entrepreneurs and social activists visualise a future that is fairer, better organised and more fulfilling before they begin to make that a reality. Sculptors look at a block of stone and say with Michaelangelo: "I see the angel in the marble and carve until I set him free." [*Expand with current or local examples.*]

When our imagination fails, hope dies

We no longer picture a positive future. Dreams collapse around us. This is what we see in the two people walking to Emmaus. They used to imagine a bright future with Jesus, but now they talk about him in the past tense: "We had hoped that he was the one who was going to redeem Israel" (Luke 24:21). In their grief and disappointment, they fail to recognise Jesus as he stands in front of them.

Jesus meets us in our mess

These two disciples were, in some ways, walking away from their faith. Walking away from where the other disciples were, away from where Jesus had died. But even as they are walking away, Jesus still joins them and walks with them. We are misled if we think that God is not interested in the messy parts of our lives, in our pain or our difficulties. When we walk away, he is present, even though we can find it hard to recognise him (see Psalm 139:11-12).

Imagination reborn

These disciples were hoping that Jesus would overthrow the Romans by military, political might. When they looked at the cross, all they could see was defeat. But on the road, Jesus transforms their way of looking at the world. Ronald Rolheiser writes:

> "Jesus appears to them on the road, listens to their discouragement, and, by restructuring their imagination and consequently their faith, he has them returning to their faith dream and their church on that same day, with the humiliation of the crucifixion now integrated into their understanding." (Ronald Rolheiser, *Sacred Fire*, pp 101-102)

As he breaks the bread, Jesus gives them new eyes to see the world, to see his suffering and their own suffering not as defeat but as the path to new life (2 Cor 4:13-18). We are God's works of art, the beautiful sculptures he is revealing by allowing setbacks and struggles to chip away at the stone-hard outer layers. We can start to re-imagine the future God has for us, for his church, for the world, a glorious future that passes through pain on the road to freedom.

RESPONSE

Contemplative Response: Resurrect Your Imagination

Ronald Rolheiser writes:

> "For all of us there will come times when everything that is precious to us religiously will get crucified and we will find ourselves discouraged, shattered religiously... this is not a crisis of faith but a crisis of the imagination... Deeper maturity and a more faithful discipleship are found on the road to Emmaus, when discouraged, in darkness, and tempted, we let our imaginations be restructured by a deeper vision of what God, Christ and the church mean." *Sacred Fire*, pages 104-105

Think about a situation where you feel like something important to your faith has died. Did you have a dream that came to nothing? Was there an aspect of doctrine or ethics that you held to with certainty, and then it began to shake? Have you been let down or disappointed by Christian sisters and brothers? In what way do you feel like those disciples on the road to Emmaus, discouraged, confused, and beginning to walk away from what you thought was important? Reflect on that, and bring how you feel about it to God.

[*Allow space for silent reflection.*]

What would happen if God restructured your imagination about that situation? They thought a crucified Messiah was a failed Messiah. Jesus showed them that crucifixion was the road to life and freedom. Ask God to show you how you can look at your disappointments differently. How can resurrection imagination change your perspective on your troubles?

[*Allow space for silent reflection.*]

Confession of Faith

This can be used as part of the communion preparation, or as a stand-alone item. It is based on part of the Emmaus story, Luke 24:19-32. Proclaim this aloud together.

We believe that Jesus was sent from God, powerful in word and deed.

Jesus was handed over by the rulers to be sentenced to death.

Jesus, the long hoped-for redeemer, was crucified.

We have heard that on the third day the women went to the tomb but didn't find his body.

They returned with stories of angels, who said he was alive.

We, like his disciples, are slow and foolish of heart, and our eyes are so often closed.

We proclaim that Jesus was the Christ who had to suffer and then enter his glory.

Jesus is the true meaning of Moses, the Prophets and the story of Israel.

Jesus walks among us, stays with us, and reveals himself as bread is broken.

Amen.

Emmaus Communion

We imagine this with the congregation seated around tables with bread rolls and wine glasses of grape juice from the beginning of the time together. However, adapt this for what will work in your setting and tradition, adding in other prayers, songs and methods of distribution as appropriate to your context.

Say: As we prepare for communion, let's enter the Emmaus story in Luke 24:13-14, on the day of Jesus' resurrection.

We read that as the two disciples walked together they were talking "about everything that had happened".

Invite: In pairs or groups, I'd like to invite you to share something from your own experience about your journey of these last few days or weeks.

[*Allow time for sharing.*]

As we read on, we see that Jesus asked the two disciples on the way to Emmaus "What are you talking about?" It says that "With sadness written across their faces, they stopped and told him of their disappointments."

In verse 21 they say "We had hoped..." I suspect we all have things in our lives that feel like that - disappointments, hopes that seem to be shattered.

Invite: Take a moment of silence to stop and tell Jesus about your disappointments. What has not worked out the way you hoped? What has seemed like tragedy? Take some time now in the silence to talk to Jesus about those things - we know from the passage that he will listen to you.

[*Allow time for silent prayer.*]

Invite: The travellers to Emmaus tell Jesus their story, and he responds by unpacking the Old Testament for them. We are going to use some of their words to join with those disciples and declare our faith in Jesus together:

Say together: [*Confession of faith on previous page.*]

Say: The story continues with the group arriving at Emmaus. Night falls, and the disciples urge Jesus to stay with them. When he is at the table he takes bread, gives thanks, breaks it, and gives it to them, and as he does so we read that their eyes are opened and they recognised him.

Let's join in that story today.

[*At this point you may wish to use other prayers and words as per your tradition, and distribute the elements as you see fit.*]

Invite: I want to invite you on your tables to take the bread, one person can pray a prayer of thanks, then please break the bread and share it together.

Once you have done that please also share the wine. Let's come expectant that Jesus will open our eyes to his presence with us as we gather around this meal together.

[*Share bread and wine.*]

Say together:

Thank you for meeting us in the breaking of bread.

Open our eyes to see you walking with us every day.

Open our ears to hear your voice in every story.

Open our hearts to burn for you, that our lives may be a living sacrifice.

Send us out in the power of your Spirit and the peace of your presence.

Amen.

SENDING

Sending Prayer

LEADER: God sends you out
to be his resurrection people!

Jesus who was dead, is now alive.
ALL: He opened our eyes to see him.

Jesus restructures our imagination.
He helps us see the world, his way.

Our hearts burn with passion in his presence.
We are sent out as his witnesses.

**God, send us out
to be your resurrection people!**

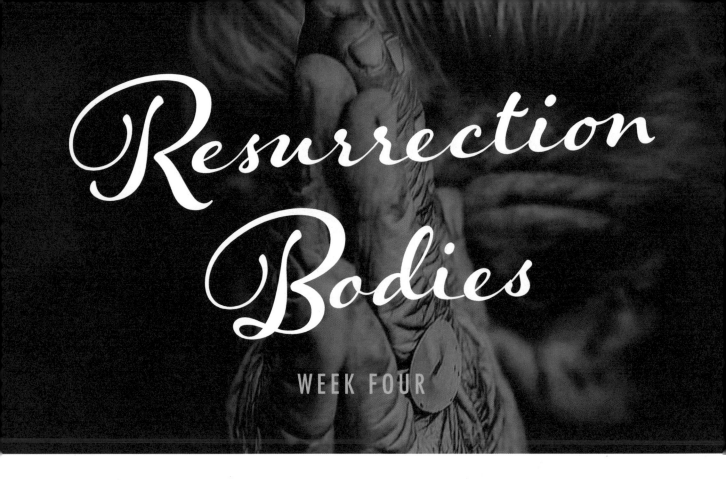

Resurrection Bodies

WEEK FOUR

FOR LEADERS

This week focuses on the nature of Jesus' risen body. He is not a dis-embodied spirit, but has a transformed physical body. This changes how we look at our own bodies, the physical world, and the hope of the transformed world to come. This week involves various ideas for "embodied worship": be sensitive towards those who have limited movement and encourage people to interpret any movements in ways appropriate for them.

GATHERING

Gathering Prayer

LEADER: Christ is risen!
ALL: He is risen indeed, hallelujah!

You stand among us, saying "Peace be with you",
we gaze in confusion, joy and amazement.
Open our minds, risen saviour,
to hear your word, and respond in faith.

Christ is risen!
He is risen indeed, hallelujah!

ALL AGE IDEAS

Everybody Needs a Body

A parody of the Blues Brothers song "Everybody Needs Somebody". This encourages us to celebrate the bodies God has given us. Show the video, or if you have confident musicians you could try performing your own version.

Body Language for Worship

An all-age talk to get people engaging their bodies.

Ask: Who here speaks French? Anyone speak Mandarin? Swahili? Any other languages spoken here? [*Welcome responses.*]

How about this: who knows "body language"? Who can understand that form of communication? Let's see, what if I say this in body language: [*fold arms, look stroppy. Let people interpret how you look.*]

How about if I look like this: [*stand stiffly to attention, feet together, saluting.*]

What am I saying if I look like this: [*slouch, one hand on hip and yawning.*]

Now, who thinks that God reads body language? Yes? I think he does. Now, he's always going to love us and accept us, whatever signals we're giving off with our body language. But I think it does make a difference, at least to us, how we come physically to God. For example, if I was going to give you some chocolate, what would you do with your body? [*People put their hands out.*]

That's right - you put your hands out, you open up your posture because you want to receive that good gift. It can be the same in worship - God wants to fill us with his love and his Holy Spirit, so in response we can put our hands out, or open up our posture, to help us receive.

What about if you wanted to tell God with your body that you were sorry - can you show me that in a posture? Yes, you might bow your head, or kneel, or even lie down. Those are all ways of saying with our bodies that we recognise that God is bigger, more important, more right than us.

How would you show God you want to praise him with your body - can you show me? Yes, maybe raising your hands, or dancing, or doing the sign language for praise.

What about if you wanted to remember Jesus on the cross, can you show me what you might do with your body for that? Yes, you might cross yourself, or push your fingers into your palms, which is the British Sign Language for the name of Jesus. There are all sorts of different ways we can worship God with our bodies. Before we move on, I want to think about how you are coming to God today... [*Download full text via engageworship.org/resurrection*]

Poem: We Like Taking Things Apart

This poem has been made into a fun video. Show this, or alternatively just get a good reader to perform the poem.

We like taking things apart
so they're distinct and separated.
We categorise, distinguish
'til they're disassociated.
Our world divides and conquers,
we dichotomize to bits,
creating camps and factions
until nothing really fits.

We say "physical" and "spiritual",
and "secular" and 'sacred",
and "normal things" and "special things"
as if they're unrelated.
There's things we think God cares about,
like spirits, souls and minds,
while bodies, work and earthly things
we guess he'd leave behind.

Yet God, our great creator,
he likes looking at the whole.
He made ourselves so integrated,
body, mind and soul.
He made the heavens and the earth
and linked it all together,
with systems, shapes and patterns
to the tides, the years, the weather.

He doesn't think we're all the same,
and yet we all belong.
We sing our different harmonies
that add up to one song.
We bring to him our whole selves,

soul and strength, and mind and heart.
He loves the total of our lives,
the sum of all our parts.

He's God the integrator.
God is three and God is one.
Forever indivisibly
the Father, Spirit, Son.
We're not just spirits in some meat,
or brains upon a pole,
so stick us back together, God,
and take our all, our whole.

MUSIC IDEAS

Songs

- *Listen To The Words Of The Risen Christ* - Joel Payne
- *Christ Was Raised* - Sam Hargreaves (page 43)
- *All I Am* - Mallory Wickham, Phil Wickham
- *Once For All* - CityAlight
- *Ain't No Grave* - Molly Skaggs, Jonathan David Helser, Melissa Helser

Hymns

- *The Hands Of Christ, The Caring Hands* - Michael Perry
- *In Resurrection Bodies* - Margaret Clarkson

HEARING GOD'S WORD

Bible Readings

Luke 24:36-49
1 Corinthians 15:12-23

Sign Language Gospel Reading

Find someone in your congregation or your wider community who is fluent in sign language. Ask them to sign the gospel reading (Luke 24:36-49) as it is being read aloud, and invite the congregation to try and join in the signs (you may need to slow the reader down). This aims to encourage solidarity with those who use sign language, and also to add a physical element to the reading.

Sermon Outline

Expand upon the following, exploring the passages. For further input read this week's Personal Devotions, and we also recommend the book "Body" by Paula Gooder.

"Resurrection" is a misunderstood word
It is easy to think that resurrection means a person will live on in spirit, that their soul will continue on like a disembodied ghost. It can be comforting to think that about our loved ones, or about Jesus. But that is not what resurrection means in the Bible. Jews who believed in resurrection took the view that, at the end of time, God would raise them in physical, bodily form. Until then, any "life after death" was either a temporary re-animation such as with Lazarus, or a ghostly encounter. Tom Wright writes:

> "Everybody knew about ghosts, spirits, visions, hallucinations and so on. Most people in the ancient world believed in some such things. They were quite clear that that wasn't what they meant by 'resurrection'... Resurrection meant bodies." *Surprised by Hope*, page 48.

Jesus' physical, transformed resurrection body
In our story today, the disciples see the risen Jesus, and they think he is a ghost. But Jesus proves that he

 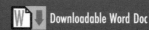

has flesh and bones - he has the marks in his hands and feet, he can eat fish. He is no ghost - he is physical. However, this body is also able to appear and disappear (Luke 24:31, 36), it is eternal and incorruptible. Jesus has a resurrected, transformed physical body.

The future now

The Jews believed that this "resurrection" was supposed to happen at the end of time (John 11:24), but Jesus drags God's future into the now. He pulls God's promised "new creation" into current life. He shows us what our own resurrection bodies, and the resurrection of all creation, will look like. Physical but transformed. Real but imperishable. Created but eternal.

Firstfruits of what's to come

This is why Paul describes the risen Jesus as the "firstfruits" (1 Cor 15:20-23). His resurrection is like those very early apples on the tree, promising us that spring is emerging and more good things are on their way. His resurrection body gives us hope that our bodies matter, that this created world matters, and that God will resurrect our bodies and his whole creation. [*Expand on the implications of this - for how we treat our current bodies, how we relate to the planet, etc.*]

RESPONSE

Active: Hand Prayers

Be sensitive to your congregation if you use this prayer, and offer alternative movements if there are people with limited movement or other issues that would hinder their ability to participate.

Explain: We're going to pray using our hands. First, rest your hands in your lap, palms facing up. See all the lines and creases in your hands, totally unique to you.

Pray: Creator God, we thank you for making us unique; that you knit us together in this beautiful way.

Explain: Next, put the tip of your right pointing finger in the centre of your left hand. Jesus' risen body still bore the marks of the nails in his hands, and he invited Thomas to touch the marks. Imagine being Thomas and feeling that physical proof of Jesus' resurrection.

Pray: Risen saviour, we thank you for your death and resurrection, conquering sin and death. We sense death and illness in our bodies, but we thank you that you promise that we will rise with you.

Explain: Next, close your hands into fists in front of you. Most of us carry baggage when it comes to our own thinking about our bodies. As you hold your fists, consider what baggage you carry: it could be your own feelings or attitudes towards your body, words spoken over you or perhaps you carry what the culture around us tells us about our bodies. Perhaps our bodies have let us down somehow, or the world we live in, not always set up for a healthy lifestyle, has let us down. Whatever baggage you are carrying, imagine holding it in your hands, and mention it in your heart to God.

Pray: Loving Father, your grace is enough for us. We let go of our burdens and ask you to carry them for us... [*Download full text via engageworship. org/resurrection*]

Contemplative: Your Body is a Temple

Optional introduction: We are going to spend a moment reflecting on a passage of Scripture from 1 Corinthians. We can read or hear Scripture in different ways - sometimes we listen for learning, like we're in a lesson, sometimes we listen for inspiration, like we would to a pep talk. Today I want to invite you to contemplate God as we hear his Word, experience it more like you would a beautiful sunset or a profound piece of art. So find a comfortable posture and take a couple of deep breaths. Find a sense of stillness within.

[*Leave some silence.*]

Say: 1 Corinthians 6:19-20 says:

"Do you not know that your bodies are temples of the Holy Spirit, who is in you, whom you have received from God? You are not your own; you were bought at a price. Therefore honour God with your bodies."

Imagine for a moment a beautiful temple, perhaps Solomon's temple in Jerusalem or perhaps the most inspiring church or chapel you've ever been in. Imagine the floor, and what the ceiling looks like too.

In the Old Testament, the presence of God rested in the temple in Jerusalem, in the holy of holies. In your imagination, in the temple you've imagined, what would the presence of God feel like? Is it a physical sensation? Can you feel it on your skin, or would you sense it with your hearing? What does the temple you're imagining smell like? What does the air feel like if you inhale through your mouth?

Take a moment to imagine the presence of God in your temple.

Now, make yourself aware of your own body. Feel the weight of yourself on the seat, sense the floor under your feet. Consider your arms and the posture of your hands. Feel how your neck and back support the weight of your head... [*Download full text via engageworship.org/resurrection*]

Intercession: Listen to the Words

Lead Joel Payne's song based on the gospel reading for today. Then allow the music to continue softly as you turn the congregation's focus to praying for others.

Explain: We've been singing those words of Jesus, "Peace be with you." Let's take a moment to think about places in the world that need God's peace. *[Give a moment for thought.]* I want to invite you to say aloud a place or situation that is on your heart. *[Let people speak.]*

Let's sing that refrain over those situations. *[Sing "Peace be with you" a few times.]*

Now let's think of places closer to here - streets, schools, businesses, or neighbourhoods in our area that need God's peace. *[Give a moment for thought.]* I want to invite you to say aloud a local place or organisation that is on your heart. *[Let people speak.]*

Let's sing that refrain over those places. *[Sing "Peace be with you" a few times.]*

Finally, think of people you know who need God's peace. *[Give a moment for thought.]* Let's speak out the first names of people who are on your heart. *[Let people speak.]*

Let's sing that refrain over those people. *[Sing "Peace be with you" a few times.]*

SENDING

Sending Prayer

LEADER: God sends you out
to be his resurrection people!

Jesus who was dead, is now alive.
ALL: He's the firstfruits of all creation.

The risen Jesus walked, talked and ate.
He showed us that our bodies are good.

Jesus has brought peace to us.
We are sent out to bring peace to creation.

**God, send us out
to be your resurrection people!**

Raising Doubts

WEEK FIVE

FOR LEADERS

This week we want to help people journey with the idea that doubt is a vital part of faith. That it is good and healthy to ask questions, challenge our assumptions, and be honest about the things we're not sure about. Thomas gives us a model of someone who spoke their doubts from the heart, but also responded to Jesus' call with faith and worship.

GATHERING

Gathering Prayer

LEADER: Christ is risen!
ALL: He is risen indeed, hallelujah!

Lord we can't see you, yet we believe in you,
meet us in our unbelief.
Help us bring our questions, risen saviour,
that we may know you as our Lord and our God.

Christ is risen!
He is risen indeed, hallelujah!

ALL AGE

Questioners in the Bible

This is an introduction to this week. If you have children or young people present, ask them to read out the verses, and make sure to include them in the group conversations. The Bible verses can be shown on the screen using the PowerPoint. You will need paper, pens and a questions box.

Say: The Bible is full of questioners.

Abraham asked God: "Sovereign Lord, how can I know that I will gain possession of the land?" (Gen 15:8)

Sarah laughed and asked: "An old woman like me? Get pregnant? With this old man of a husband?" (Gen 18:12, MSG)

Moses asked of God: "Who am I that I should go to Pharaoh and bring the Israelites out of Egypt?" (Ex 3:11)

The Psalmist asked: "Why, Lord, do you stand far off? Why do you hide yourself in times of trouble?" (Psalm 10:1)

The disciples asked Jesus: "When will these things happen that you have told us about?" (Mark 13:4)

And Thomas, being told that Jesus was risen and had appeared to the disciples, responded by saying: "Unless I see the nail marks in his hands and put my finger where the nails were, and put my hand into his side, I will not believe." (John 20:25)

Sometimes, people can think that if we have faith in God then we will have no questions. But faith and doubt need to work together. When we have faith, we need to believe beyond what we can see. And sometimes that will mean asking questions, being curious, being inquisitive, like Sarah and Moses and Thomas were.

Talk in groups: what are some questions you would like to ask God?

Write them down and post them in a questions box.

Explain: We're not planning to look through these questions and answer them. The reason to write them down is just to bring these questions to God, being honest about them. Some questions God will answer, at some point. Other times we might need to keep wrestling with them, and choose to believe even when we don't have clear answers in front of us. Jesus said to Thomas:

"Because you have seen me, you have believed; blessed are those who have not seen and yet have believed." (John 20:29)

The FOMO Game

Ask for some volunteers and bring them to the front. Choose how many: it could be just one confident person, if they're young people they might want to be a little team. They probably need to be over 11 years old.

Explain that they need to look very carefully around them, because when they come back into the room, lots of things will have changed.

Ask an assistant to take the volunteer(s) out of the room. If you have a side-room or vestry that would be ideal, but make sure that they can't hear what's being said in the main meeting room. Noise-cancelling headphones

and some music may be necessary.

While your volunteer(s) are out of the room, enact some events that would be spottable for people with attention to detail. You'll need to adapt this to your circumstances, but here are some ideas:

> *Move the lectern to the other side of the church.*
> *The Pastor and their spouse swap jumpers.*
> *Everyone turn their chair and face to the right.*
> *Flowers are replaced by Christmas decorations or something else out of place.*
> *Everyone wearing glasses takes them off.*
> *Put something silly on the projection screen.*
> *Instruments on platform swap places.*
> *Replace choir conductor with a teddy bear... etc.*

Act fast with these changes, and then bring the volunteer(s) in. Ask them if they can work out what has happened while they've been out of the room. Award a point/sticker/sweet for each change they spot.

Interview volunteer(s): What do you think happened while you were out of the room? How did it feel to not get to be part of that? When you came back into the room, how did you notice that stuff had been happening while you were out?

Explain: In John 20, we read about the resurrected Jesus appearing to his group of disciples, but Thomas wasn't there! Can you imagine leaving the room for a moment, then coming back, not just to the chairs facing a different way, but to hear us say "Jesus was here, in bodily form, while you were out!".

I wonder if Thomas developed some FOMO - Fear Of Missing Out? Perhaps he never left the other disciples' sides again!

Interview volunteer(s): What do you think Thomas noticed when he came back into the room? Do you think he could sense what had happened? How do you think Thomas felt?

[Perhaps end with an applause for your volunteer(s).]

MUSIC IDEAS

Songs

- *Jesus Only You* - Timo Scharnowski (printed on page 42)
- *My Lighthouse* - Rend Collective
- *I've Had Questions* - Tim Hughes
- *Lay It All Down (At The Feet Of Jesus)* - Freddie Washington/Will Reagan
- *Christ Is Risen, He Is Risen Indeed* - Keith Getty, Kristyn Getty, Ed Cash

Hymns:

- *We Have Not Seen Thy Footsteps Tread, or modernised version We Were Not There To See You Come* - Ann Richter and John H Gurney
- *When Thomas Heard From Jesus* - Carolyn Winfrey Gillette

HEARING GOD'S WORD

Bible Readings

John 20:19-31
1 Peter 1:3-9

Active Reading John 20 - Jesus is Alive

By Bob Hartman

Telling tips - point to the congregation and have them say/shout the "Jesus is alive!" line when it appears. This is part of the text - download the full script via the link at the bottom of this page.

Jesus is alive.

It's evening, the first day of the week, and the disciples are together, behind locked doors; still in fear of the Jewish leaders.

Jesus is alive.

And they know it, because, suddenly, there he is standing among them! "Shalom," he says.

Just an ordinary greeting.

But there's nothing ordinary about this moment, as he shows them his hands and his side.

The disciples are overjoyed.

Jesus is alive.

"Shalom," he says again. "Peace be with you."

And then he gives them a job. "My Father sent me," he says. "Now I am sending you."

And he gives them what they need for the job, by breathing on them... [*Download full script from engageworship.org/resurrection*]

Sermon Outline

Expand upon the following, exploring the passages. For further input read this week's Personal Devotions, and we also recommend "When Everything's On Fire" by Brian Zahnd.

"Are you sure about that?"

We might hear that question from our loved ones, or from our computer when we're about to delete a load of files. It is the voice of healthy doubt, causing us to pause, question, re-evaluate. This can be really helpful and can save you a lot of problems! [*You may have a story from your life to illustrate this.*]

Today we've heard about Thomas, who often gets called "doubting Thomas". Sometimes we can feel as if doubt is the opposite to faith. However, another approach is to see that doubt is actually a vital part of faith.

Healthy things change

Healthy living things do not stay the same, they grow, change, adapt. As we go through the life of faith, God will be at work, refining our beliefs. If we never doubt or question, we will never be open to the changes God wants to bless us with. Dostoevsky wrote:

> "I believe in Christ and confess him not like some child; my hosanna has passed through an enormous furnace of doubt." Quoted in Brian Zahnd, *When Everything's On Fire*, page 23.

Thomas is a good example of someone whose beliefs changed for the better through doubt. As a good Jew, he did not believe that a person could be raised from the dead this side of the end of the world. At least, if it was true he wanted to see the proof. Thomas was the kind of person who said what he felt (see John 11:16, 14:5), he was honest about his questions and didn't hide them.

Doubt your doubts

Author Graham Greene confessed to having mixed feelings about religion and Christianity. However, he told one journalist that:

> "When he read the story in John's gospel of the two disciples racing each other to the empty tomb after Christ's body had disappeared, he felt that it was 'authentic reportage'. It was this, he went on, that 'enabled me to doubt my doubt about the resurrection'."
> John Cornwell "The Importance of Doubt"
> www.theguardian.com/world/2007/aug/30/religion.uk

Like Graham Greene, like Thomas, we should not push down our doubts. Instead, we should "doubt our doubts", hold them up to the light, hold them up to God. Talk to trusted friends about the ideas you struggle with. Listen to a variety of perspectives. Allow God to take you deeper into them.

Choosing to believe

Jesus doesn't reject Thomas for doubting. He comes with the proof Thomas has asked for. And Thomas, true to his character, immediately allows Jesus to transform his thinking. He obeys Jesus' instruction, admitting that the time for doubting this belief is over. He worships Jesus as his Lord and his God. There will come times when you and I have choices like this. We may not have all our doubts removed. We may not be able to see the fullness of the answers we seek but, having doubted well, we are then invited to take a step of faith and to choose to believe deeper in Jesus.

RESPONSE

Contemplative: Own Your Doubts, Cast Your Burdens

Invite people to close their eyes. Lead this in a reflective fashion.

Imagine for a moment that you're walking along a dark path at night. Out of the corner of your eye, you see something shadowy moving just off the path. How do you feel about that shadowy movement? What do you do about it?

Sometimes, doubts are like shadows on a dark path. If you let them stay on the periphery of your vision, you can start to get quite scared about them. However, if you address them head on, go and look at them, you will most often discover that they're not as scary as they seem. On a dark path the shadows might just be a tree, a bush or some other harmless thing. When you look at your doubts directly, their power diminishes.

What doubts do you have in the periphery of your vision right now? It might be to do with your faith, or the resurrection in particular. It might be another issue of belief or ethics, or something to do with your family, job or health. If you feel able to, bring one of those doubts into the light and consider it head on for a moment. Own the fact that this doubt exists.

Bring that doubt to God in prayer. Talk to him about it.

What do you feel God might be saying about that?... [*Download full text via engageworship. org/resurrection*]

Active: Speaking Blessings

This is an active response, asking everyone to stand up and get involved in blessing one another.

Explain: To speak blessing means to speak a "good word" over someone. A word of encouragement, truth, kindness, grace. On the screen are a list of potential blessings - you might be able to think of others. Walk around and speak a blessing over people you come across. Receive blessings from others.

Blessed are you who have not seen and yet have believed.

Blessed are you when you don't push down your questions, but speak out your doubts.

Blessed are you who don't have all the answers, yet dare to walk in faith.

Blessed are you who would love things to be certain, but bravely face the unpredictable.

Blessed are you when life takes an unexpected turn, and you hold on to Jesus for dear life.

Blessed are you who reject rigid, easy answers and embrace living, growing, challenging questions.

Blessed are you when you know you are poor in spirit, for yours is the kingdom of heaven.

Blessed are you who mourn, for you will be comforted.

Blessed are the meek, for you will inherit the earth.

Blessed are you who hunger and thirst for righteousness, for you will be filled.

Blessed are the merciful, for you will be shown mercy.

Blessed are the pure in heart, for you will see God.

Blessed are the peacemakers, for you will be called children of God.

Blessed are you who are persecuted because of righteousness, for yours is the kingdom of heaven.

Song: Jesus Only You

This new song emerges from the stories of the disciples and Thomas. It expresses their struggles and doubts, then turns in faith to say that only Jesus will satisfy, that he is "our Lord and our God".

Have your musicians lead the song (lead sheet on page 42), or make use of the lyric video.

Even though the walls are up,
even though the doors are locked,
you give your peace to us
again and again.

SENDING

Sending Prayer

LEADER: God sends you out
to be his resurrection people!

Jesus who was dead, is now alive.
ALL: We believe, help our unbelief.

We'd like to touch his hands and see proof.
We have faith in what we haven't seen.

The risen Jesus comforts us in our doubt.
We are sent out into a doubting world.

**God, send us out
to be your resurrection people!**

Restoring Work

WEEK SIX

INTRO FOR LEADERS

In this session we explore how the risen Jesus blessed the work the disciples were doing, even in the midst of their frustration. We'll see how work is a part of resurrection life, both now and for eternity.

Think about how you can affirm the different kinds of work people will do - paid and unpaid, fulfilling and challenging.

GATHERING

Gathering Prayer

LEADER: Christ is risen!
ALL: He is risen indeed, hallelujah!

We gather from our weeks of work,
whether they feel fruitful, frustrating, or fulfilling.
You meet us in our work, risen saviour,
and welcome every task as an offering of worship.

Christ is risen!
He is risen indeed, hallelujah!

ALL AGE

Poem - Work Can Be A Burden

Perform this poem confidently. Teach the refrain so that everyone can join in.

**Work can be a burden,
work can be a chore,
but when we work with Jesus,
our work can be much more.**

Back in the beginning,
when all the world was made,
Eve and Adam worked there,
as partners, not as slaves.

They gave names to the creatures,
they cared for plants and birds,
their work was good and helpful,
respectful of God's world.

Work can be a burden...

But then temptation struck us,
we chose to disobey,
we hid from our creator:
we caused him real dismay.

"Where are you?" called our maker,
"what have you done?" he cried.
"Now work will be a toil,
the ground has been defiled."

Work can be a burden...

The gift that had been given
has turned into a curse,
and those who work get cheated,
frustrated, bored and worse.

But Jesus' resurrection
reverses Eden's fall,
and promises a new day:
this curse will be no more.

Work can be a burden...

Our work can take on meaning,
it can be good and free,
a blessing to the planet,
a gift to those in need.

God uses all our passions,
our efforts and our skills,
to see all nations prosper
and households pay their bills.

So whether it's a garden,
an office or a school,
a kitchen or a factory,
a park or swimming pool,

your workplace is for worship,
your labour's not in vain.
Let's work alongside Jesus
and see his world remade.

Work can be a burden...

This Time Tomorrow

This is a simple little idea from the London Institute for Contemporary Christianity. If you use this idea, consider making it a monthly feature in your church, as it is a wonderful tool for helping us think about our work differently over time.

Interview a member of the congregation, asking these questions:

> *Where will you be "This Time Tomorrow?"*
> *What do you do there?*
> *What are your challenges and joys?*
> *How can we pray for you?*

If you only do this once, it would perhaps be helpful to interview three very different people: for example, someone in paid full-time work, someone who's retired and someone who is a student.

To read more about the thinking behind this idea, go to: licc.org.uk/resources/this-time-tomorrow/

MUSIC IDEAS

Songs

- *Christ Was Raised* - Sam Hargreaves (page 43)
- *In The Light Of Your Mercy* - Sam Hargreaves
- *We Bring Our Time (God The Maker)* - The Porter's Gate
- *Before You I Kneel (A Worker's Prayer)* - Keith Getty, Kristyn Getty, Stuart Townend, Jeff Taylor
- *Christ Be In My Waking* - Stuart Townend, Simon Brading

Hymns:

- *We Seek Your Kingdom* - Andy Flannagan, Graham Hunter, Noel Robinson
- *Take My Life And Let It Be* - Frances Ridley Havergal

- *Forth In Thy Name* - Charles Wesley
- *Be The God Of All My Sundays* - Martin Leckebusch

HEARING GOD'S WORD

Bible Readings

John 21:1-14
Isaiah 65:17-25

John 21 Active Reading

Invite people to repeat what you say and do. So for the first line, say the line while doing the action, and then the congregation do and say the same along with you.

Working as a fisherman *[mime casting rod]*.
We've got blisters on our hands *[show hands]*.
We've been fishing through the night *[yawn]*,
yet there are no fish in sight *[hold up empty hands, look sad]*.

Someone standing on the beach *[shade eyes and squint to make out]*.
Calls to us "you got no fish?" *[hold hands around mouth to shout louder]*.
Give our weary heads a shake *[shake heads]*.
Nothing seems to go our way *[thumbs down]*.

Stranger says "why don't you try *[hold hands around mouth to shout louder]*
casting on the other side?" *[point to the right]*.
Heard those words somewhere before *[scratch head, look puzzled]*,
we obey and fish once more *[throw net on right side]*.

Suddenly our nets are full *[arms up, shocked face]*,
too much for our arms to pull! *[try pulling nets hard]*.
I look at that guy again *[shade eyes and squint to make out]*,
"Hey it's Jesus, it's our friend!" *[point in delight]*.

Peter leaps into the sea *[mime dive]*,
swims to Jesus, full of glee *[mime swim, silly grin]*.
Leaving us to land the boat *[wipe sweat off brow]*,
all these fish, it barely floats! *[bend knees as if sinking]*.

On the beach we find a camp *[point]*,
coalfire glows to dry the damp *[warm hands]*.
Jesus says "give me those fish" *[hand out]*
cooks them for our breakfast dish *[mime frying pan]*.

Risen Jesus, here today *[point at everyone]*,
be in all we do and say *[bring your hands to your heart]*.
Take the work our hands produce *[hold open hands]*,
put it to eternal use *[lift hands to heaven]*.

Sermon Outline

Expand upon the following, exploring the passages. For further input read this week's Personal Devotions, and we also recommend "Garden City" by John Mark Comer.

Unexpected Place to Meet

Where do you expect to meet with the risen Jesus? In a church service, or in your personal prayer time? At a Christian conference, or walking through a beautiful landscape? In our story today, Jesus meets his disciples in a very unexpected place. So unexpected that, like we've seen in lots of our stories before, his friends don't recognise him. Imagine him showing up at your desk, or your classroom, or on your building site, or by your breakfast table. Would you recognise him?

Failure at Work

In this story, Jesus literally turns up at Peter's workplace. And he turns up on a day when Peter is feeling a failure. The very thing Peter thought he could do - be a fisherman - is the thing he's drawing a blank on. No fish. Not even a nibble. But notice - Jesus doesn't rebuke Peter and the disciples for returning to fishing. In fact, he encourages and helps them. Work, it turns out, is good. Work is part of the resurrection life Jesus has risen again to bring us. He doesn't call us all to stop work and just be spiritual for the rest of our lives (and on into eternity). He comes alongside us in our work, and breathes his life into it.

A Vision of Eternity

Back in Isaiah 65, the prophet painted a picture of the "new heavens and new earth" God was going to recreate at the end of time. And the picture is not of clouds and angels playing harps. It's not the endless church services some of us have in our heads! He says:

> They will build houses and dwell in them; they will plant vineyards and eat their fruit.
>
> No longer will they build houses and others live in them, or plant and others eat...
>
> my chosen ones will long enjoy the work of their hands.
>
> They will not labour in vain. (Is 65:21-23)

God will not do away with work, but he will banish futile work. Unjust work. Vain work. The promise of eternity is a heavenly city on earth where we enjoy all God's good gifts, including food, houses, and satisfying, enjoyable work. Does that vision change how you view your work now? Jesus wants to come alongside us, even when things are frustrating or difficult, and breathe life into our work, breathe some of those qualities of resurrection into what we're doing right now.

Breakfast on the Beach

When we work with Jesus, he can bring abundant results. 153 fish is a huge catch, far more than they needed or expected. Submitting the work of our hands to God can lead to him doing "immeasurably more than all we ask or imagine, according to his power that is at work within us" (Eph 3:20).

And Jesus can take the fruit of our work, as he took those fish, and use it. We can gather around the breakfast campfire with Jesus and enjoy the harvest of his grace in our work.

RESPONSE

Contemplative Response: Unexpected Places

Invite people to close their eyes. Lead this in a reflective fashion.

Jesus showed up in an unexpected place. He appeared in the disciples' place of work, and they didn't recognise him. He helped them with their work, and they responded a little like Jacob back in Genesis 28: "Surely the LORD was in this place, and I was not aware of it."

Picture somewhere you go in your week. Somewhere you least expect to meet Jesus. It could be at work, at school, or on your commute. It could be with a particular person, or at a shop, pub or community centre you go to. It could be on a specific street, or it could even be in your home.

Choose one place, and picture it as vividly as you can.

> Are you sitting, standing or walking?
>
> What does it look like around you? What details can you see?
>
> What can you hear?
>
> What can you smell?
>
> Is there anyone else there?
>
> How do you feel about being in that place?
>
> Now imagine Jesus comes into that situation.
>
> What do you think Jesus would do - would he sit down, walk with you, how would he be present in that space?
>
> What do you think Jesus would say?
>
> How does Jesus' presence change how you feel about that situation?

Jesus, as we bring this reflection to a close, we thank you that you have promised to be with us in every situation. You said you will never leave us or forsake us. Help us to recognise you with us during our week, and draw strength from your presence. Amen.

Intercessions: Isaiah 65

**ALL: God promises to create
a new heavens and new earth,
where we will build houses and dwell in them.**

LEADER: God we pray for those
who do not have homes,
and those who are unsafe or unwelcome
in the places they live.
Bless and inspire people in the building trade,
and people who sell and rent houses,
that their work would be done safely,
with justice and joy.

**God promises to create
a new heavens and new earth,
where we will plant vineyards
and eat their fruit.**

We pray for those who do not have enough to eat,
and those who struggle with eating disorders and
diet problems.
Bless and inspire people in agriculture,
workers in supply chains and food shops,
that food will be provided fairly and for the good
of the planet.

**God promises to create
a new heavens and new earth,
where we will enjoy the work of our hands
and our labour will not be in vain.**

We pray for those who are looking for work,
and those who find their work futile,
fruitless or overwhelming.
Bless and inspire everyone in employment,
and those who work in the home and the community,
that every task can be done for your glory and in
your presence.

**God promises to create
a new heavens and new earth,
and that we will be glad and rejoice forever in
what he will make. Amen.**

Active Response: My Fish

*Print out fish outlines on A5 paper. Give each person a
fish outline and a pen.*

Explain: In the story of the feeding of the five
thousand, the boy brings his two loaves and five
small fish to Jesus. Jesus takes them and multiplies
them, so there is enough for thousands to eat.

In our story today, this happens almost in reverse.
Jesus helps the disciples catch hundreds of fish. Then
he takes just a few, cooks them and serves them for
breakfast.

Either way, a simple principle can be learned from
both stories: give Jesus your fish! The disciples
were fishermen - the result of their work was fish.
The result of the boy (or his parent's) work was a
packed lunch. Neither may have felt or looked very
important. But Jesus was willing to take the results of
their work and use them.

Reflect: What are the results of your work? Whether
in the office, at school, in your home, on the streets
or somewhere else, we all do work and that work
produces results. The risen Jesus is able to take our
fish, the results of our work, and use them for his
glory and to build his Kingdom... [*Download full
text via engageworship.org/resurrection*]

SENDING

Sending Prayer

LEADER: God sends you out
to be his resurrection people!

Jesus who was dead, is now alive.
**ALL: He brings his resurrection power to our
everyday.**

He ushers in a new creation of fruitful work.
He affirms the goodness of our daily work.

The risen Jesus empowers us.
We are sent out to work for his glory.

**God, send us out
to be your resurrection people!**

Ascension Sunday

WEEK SEVEN

FOR LEADERS

This is the final session of the series, although you may also think of it as a prelude to Pentecost next week. It explores the significance of Jesus' ascension, and that recognising Jesus' absence can be as important as highlighting his presence.

GATHERING

Gathering Prayer

LEADER: Christ is risen!
ALL: He is risen indeed, hallelujah!

We gather to wait with your disciples,
expectant of your presence, longing for your return.
Give us patience and power, ascended saviour,
to live as your resurrection people.

Christ is risen!
He is risen indeed, hallelujah!

Testimonies

As this is the final week of the Resurrection People series, it is a good time to find out how these themes are impacting your congregation's lives. You could do this in a variety of ways - for example, you could invite people to share 60 second video testimonies of how they have experienced being Resurrection People in their everyday lives, and then edit those stories together.

Or you could interview a handful of people who have seen new life springing up in their work, school or home contexts. Or, give everyone a slip of paper with "He is not here" on one side, inviting them to write down a situation where they struggled to know Jesus' presence, and "He is here" on the other side, to write down how Jesus has been real to them in the past few weeks.

ALL AGE

Drama - Looking Up

By Dave Hopwood

[Person 1 enters, stands still and starts looking up. Person 2 walks past, sees them, stops, starts looking up as well. Person 3 enters, looks at them, shrugs and walks off, then returns and joins them in looking up. People 4 & 5 come on and join them all looking up...]

For all free downloads plus song and hymn links, visit www.engageworship.org/resurrection using password on page 2.

33

6. [*walks on*] What are you doing?

5. Looking up.

6. Why?

5. Don't know, expecting something I suppose. Ask them.

6. What are you doing?

3. Looking up.

6. Why?

3. Don't know, expecting something I suppose. Ask them.

6. What are you doing?

2. Looking up.

6. Why?

2. Don't know, expecting something I suppose. Ask them.

6. What are you doing?

1. Looking up.

6. Why?

1. Waiting. For Jesus... [*Download full text via engageworship.org/resurrection*]

Special Delivery

Prepare a postbox with a cross-shaped hole in the front, and some paper and pens. This could also be used as a response activity.

Have someone read this passage aloud:

> "Christ Jesus who died - more than that, who was raised to life - is at the right hand of God and is also interceding for us." (Rom 8:34b)

Explain: Today we are thinking about Jesus ascending back to heaven. It may be true that Jesus' earthly work was finished, but that doesn't mean he has stopped helping us! This verse says that the risen Jesus is now at the right hand side of Father God and is "interceding" for us?

Ask: What does "interceding" mean?

Explain: An intercessor is a go between, a mediator, someone who acts on our behalf. We often use the word in church when we talk about praying for other people. We intercede, praying to God for them.

Jesus is now our intercessor at God the Father's side. He is praying for me and you! Not only that,

when you or I pray, it goes through Jesus. When we sing worship songs, or serve God in our lives, it goes through Jesus. Jesus takes our prayers, our songs, our acts of service. He makes them perfect and offers them to the Father on our behalf. So we can have confidence when we come to God with prayers, or songs, or in our everyday lives, knowing that Jesus is like our heavenly postman, bringing all our offerings to our Father.

On your piece of paper, write down one thing you want Jesus to take to the Father. It could be a prayer asking for something. It could be some words of praise or thanks. It could be an offering of service you want to give to God. Write it on the paper, and post it through the cross-shaped hole into this box, as a sign that you know Jesus will take your offering to the Father.

MUSIC IDEAS

Songs

- *Before The Throne Of God Above* - Vikki Cooke
- *Jesus, Lead Us To The Father* - Sam Hargreaves
- *High In The Heavens* - Judy Gresham
- *Soon And Very Soon* - Andrae Crouch

Hymns:

- *Christ In Majesty Ascending* - David Mowbray
- *Since Our Great High Priest, Christ Jesus* - Christopher Idle
- *Ascended Christ, Who Gained* - Christopher Idle
- *Lo! In Heaven, Jesus Sitting* - Witness Lee
- *A Hymn Of Glory Let Us Sing* - trans. Benjamin Webb

HEARING GOD'S WORD

Bible Readings

Acts 1:1-11
Hebrews 4:14-16

Ascension Day Dramatic Monologue

Ideally, get a good reader to perform this. There is also an MP3 recording of an actor performing it which you could play.

Whooosh! Just like that! Like a rocket, Zoooomm, that's how he went! Better than any fireworks I've ever seen! Wheeeee! And we were watching to see where he was going when a cloud came across, and, well, that was it. Gone. Ascended.

I didn't want him to go. He'd already left us once, and that was awful. We just didn't know what to do with ourselves, we moped around, fearful for our lives, fearful for our sanity. I mean, he was our hope, we'd left everything for him. And he had promised that he would never leave us or forsake us. So when he died, what did that mean? Wasn't he who we thought he was? Was he a fake or a fool, or even a fiend? So many questions and doubts. We needed him, he was showing us the way, the way to be human, to live without the legalism of the Pharisees or the rule or the Romans. But it was just those things, the rules and the rule, which caused his death. I just didn't understand.

Then he came back. He came back! Who has ever come back from the dead?! (Well, except Lazarus, and that little girl, and... er, well, perhaps I should have trusted him a bit more.) Anyway he rose again just like he said he would. And he gave us convincing proofs he was alive, showing us his wounds and eating fish and everything! I mean, ghosts don't eat fish, do they? And he spoke to us about the Kingdom of God, and it all started to make sense, all that stuff we'd heard before but hadn't really grasped until, well, until he'd died I guess.

One time when we were eating he said "Do not leave Jerusalem, but wait for the gift my Father promised, which you have heard me speak about. For John baptised with water, but in a few days you will be baptised with the Holy Spirit."

I got all excited and said "Lord, Lord are you at this time going to restore the Kingdom of Israel?"

He looked at me in his way which means "you haven't quite got it yet, have you?" I'm getting used to that look.

He said "It's not for you to know the times and dates the Father has set for his own authority. But you will receive power when the Holy Spirit comes on you, and you will be my witnesses in Jerusalem, and in all Judea and Samaria, and to the ends of the earth."... *[Download full text via engageworship.org/resurrection]*

Sermon Outline

Expand upon the following, exploring the passages. For further input read this week's Personal Devotions, plus we also recommend "Jesus Ascended" by GS Dawson.

Presence and absence

If you have ever taught a child to ride a bike, you may remember running alongside them, holding on to the saddle. Then there comes a point when you have to let go. This can be scary and painful, but they will never learn to ride that bike until we remove our control. *[Insert your own story here.]* Similarly, when someone leaves a job or a role we can get very worried that no-one will be able to fill their shoes. Yet, often enough, their absence creates an opportunity for others to step up, for teams to be formed or new avenues to be explored. Absence can be as important as presence.

Good to go

The resurrection led to a forty day period where Jesus appeared to his disciples. Then, at the ascension, it seems that he disappears again. It may have felt to the disciples as if Jesus was abandoning them. However, Jesus had already told them that his leaving was for their benefit:

"But very truly I tell you, it is for your good that I am going away. Unless I go away, the Advocate will not come to you; but if I go, I will send him to you." (John 16:7)

Sometimes, churches can be so keen to emphasise Jesus' presence that we neglect to be honest about the fact that he is not physically with us; not in the way he will be when he returns. We need to be real about the fact that we don't always sense him with us the way we want to.

> "The great mystery of the divine revelation is that God entered into intimacy with us not only by Christ's coming, but also by his leaving... As we become aware of his absence we discover his presence, and as we realise that he left us we also come to know that he did not leave us alone." Henri Nouwen, *The Living Reminder*, pages 255, 259.

In-filled and empowered

In John 16, Jesus goes on to say that only when he goes will the Holy Spirit be poured out. This is the same power that raised Jesus from the dead and lifted Jesus to the Father in the ascension (Eph 1:19-20). Jesus' leaving opens the door to his presence filling the disciples, multiplying his ministry through them and ultimately to millions of people across the world. This is the same Holy Spirit who empowers us today, to be like Jesus to the world around us. [*You could say that you will be exploring this more next week on Pentecost Sunday.*]

A high priest who knows our weakness

The ascension makes the way for the Spirit to come, but it also assures us that Jesus has taken his humanity to heaven with him. Jesus does not forget his experiences of life on earth, instead we have a sympathetic "high priest", who sits at God the Father's right hand and brings our prayers, our cries, our failures to him:

> "Therefore, since we have a great high priest who has ascended into heaven, Jesus the Son of God, let us hold firmly to the faith we profess. For we do not have a high priest who is unable to feel sympathy for our weaknesses, but we have one who has been

tempted in every way, just as we are – yet he did not sin." (Heb 4:14-15)

His ascension gives us a sure hope that our prayers are heard by one who understands what it means to be human. His bodily resurrection and ascension encourage us to hold on in the middle of struggles and challenges, because Jesus sympathises and draws us close in our times of need.

RESPONSE

Contemplative Response: Questions for Jesus

Just before Jesus returns to heaven, one of the disciples asks him this question.

> "Lord, are you at this time going to restore the kingdom to Israel?" (Acts 1:6)

You see, Israel was under the military rule of the Romans. Imagine if another country had invaded the UK [*substitute your own country here*], and had been ruling over us at gunpoint for years. We might ask a similar thing of God - are you going to free us yet?

Of course, that isn't the case right now. But we might have similar questions. God, when are you going to sort out the politics in this country? When are you going to make things fairer for the poor? When are you going to make schools better, or fix the healthcare crisis, or heal the environment. Can you think of things like that you would want to ask Jesus?

[*Pause for reflection.*]

Or your question for Jesus might be more personal. Lord, are you at this time going to sort out this relationship? Or get me the job I want? Or heal my sickness? Or fix my money problems? What kind of questions like that might you ask Jesus?

[*Pause for reflection.*]

Interestingly, Jesus doesn't reject their question. It is not that he doesn't care about the fate of Israel. But he does have another perspective. He responds:

> "It is not for you to know the times or dates the Father has set by his own authority. But you will receive power when the Holy Spirit comes on you; and you will be my witnesses in Jerusalem, and in all Judea and Samaria, and to the ends of the earth." (Acts 1:7-8)

We are not to know the final date when Jesus will return and the earth will be restored to how God intended it. But in the meantime, Jesus promises something else. He says that the Holy Spirit, the same power that raised him from the dead, will be given to us. That we will be witnesses to him, in words and deeds, spreading the good news of his Kingdom to those around us, those further afield, and to the whole world.

Go back in your mind to the questions you thought you would ask Jesus. If Jesus was filling you with his Holy Spirit, how might he use you to be even just a tiny part of the answer to those questions? What would it look like for you to be filled with his resurrection power, and making a difference in the things which you are passionate about in the world?

[*Pause for reflection.*]

Prayer from Ephesians 1

Explain: Ephesians 1:18-23 is Paul's prayer for the church, that they would know the risen, ascended Jesus who is now in authority over all things. I'm going to pray a version of that prayer over you. Receive this ancient blessing, first written 2000 years ago and just as relevant for us today.

I pray
that the eyes of your heart
are filled with hope.
I pray
you will know just how rich
you are in Christ.
I pray
for the power that raised Christ
back from the dead.
I pray
that you know Christ, ascended,
to God's right hand.
I pray
you will know he is raised above
all names and powers.
I pray
you will know Jesus who fills
everything in every way.

Now having received that blessing, I want you to think of one other person or situation that also needs to know Jesus as the risen, ascended one. I'll pray the prayer line by line, and I invite you to repeat after me as a prayer for the person or situation that is on your heart.

SENDING

Sending Prayer

LEADER: God sends you out
to be his resurrection people!

Jesus who was dead, is now alive.
ALL: He ascended and is seated at the right hand of the Father.

His physical absence increases his presence within us.
He has not left us alone.

The risen Jesus asks us to go.
We are sent out to bring God's good news to the world.

God, send us out to be your resurrection people!

DRAW NEAR THE TOMB (RESURRECTION DAY)

Sam Hargreaves

EASTER DOESN'T STOP

Timo Scharnowski

♩ = 110

D G A D G

Ea - ster does-n't stop on Fri - day, when Je - sus died for you and
Ea - ster does-n't stop on Sa - tur-day, when Je - sus lay dead in his
Ea - ster does-n't stop on Sun - day, when Je - sus walked out of the
Ea - ster is a new beg - gin - ning, to fix what's bro - ken in this

A Bm A/C♯ D/F♯ G

me,   when he gave his life as a sac - ri - fice: but
grave,   when the peo - ple thought was he real - ly God? But
tomb.   What a great sur - prise, he was raised to life! But
world.   Sing it loud to - day, Je - sus made a way. Yeah

A D 1.

Ea - ster does - n't stop there.
Ea - ster does - n't stop there.
Ea - ster does - n't stop there.
Ea - ster does - n't stop here.

2. CHORUS

D A Bm G A D

So I won't stop ei - ther tel - ling the whole great sto - ry of Ea-ster. No

A Bm G

I won't stop ei - ther, li - ving out the true sto - ry of

A D D/F♯ A D D/F♯ A D

Ea - ster.

Actions video, lyric video and chord sheet available from engageworship.org/resurrection
Words and music © Timo Scharnowski, admin. ChurchSongs.co.uk
Please remember to report any photocopies on your CCL license. CCLI # 7190357.

IN CHRIST, NEW CREATION

Sam Hargreaves

Lyric video, actions video and chord chart available from engageworship.org/resurrection
Words and music © Sam Hargreaves admin. ChurchSongs.co.uk
Please remember to report any photocopies on your CCL license. CCLI # 7190186.

LORD IT'S HARD TO RECOGNISE YOU

Sam Hargreaves

Lyric video and chord sheet available from engageworship.org/resurrection
Words and music © Sam Hargreaves, admin. ChurchSongs.co.uk
Please remember to report any photocopies on your CCL license. CCLI # 7190187.

JESUS ONLY YOU

Timo Scharnowski

Lyric video and chord chart available from engageworship.org/resurrection
Words and music © Timo Scharnowski admin. ChurchSongs.co.uk
Please remember to report any photocopies on your CCL license. CCLI # 7190358.